Our Teacher's in a Wheelchair

Story and Pictures by Mary Ellen Powers

Albert Whitman & Company, Morton Grove, Illinois

J E

Design by Meyer Seltzer.
Cover photo and photos for pp. 9, 13, and 14 by C. G. Grant.
Photo for p. 7 by Ohio State University Department of Photography and Cinema.

Library of Congress Cataloging-in-Publication Data

Powers, Mary Ellen.
    Our teacher's in a wheelchair.

    Summary: Text and photographs depict the activities of
Brian Hanson, who is able to lead an active existence as a
nursery school teacher despite a partial paralysis requiring
the use of a wheelchair.
    1. Hanson, Brian—Juvenile literature. 2. Nursery
school teachers—United States—Biography—Juvenile
literature. 3. Handicapped teachers—United States—
Biography—Juvenile literature. 4. Day care centers—
Ohio—Upper Arlington—Case studies—Juvenile
literature. [1. Paraplegics. 2. Physically handicapped.
3. Handicapped teachers. 4. Hanson, Brian] I. Title.
II. Title: Our teacher is in a wheelchair.
LA2317.H418P69   1986   372.11'0092'4   86-1623
ISBN 0-8075-6240-8 (lib. bdg.)

This is dedicated to the one I love.

Brian Hanson teaches in a day-care center.

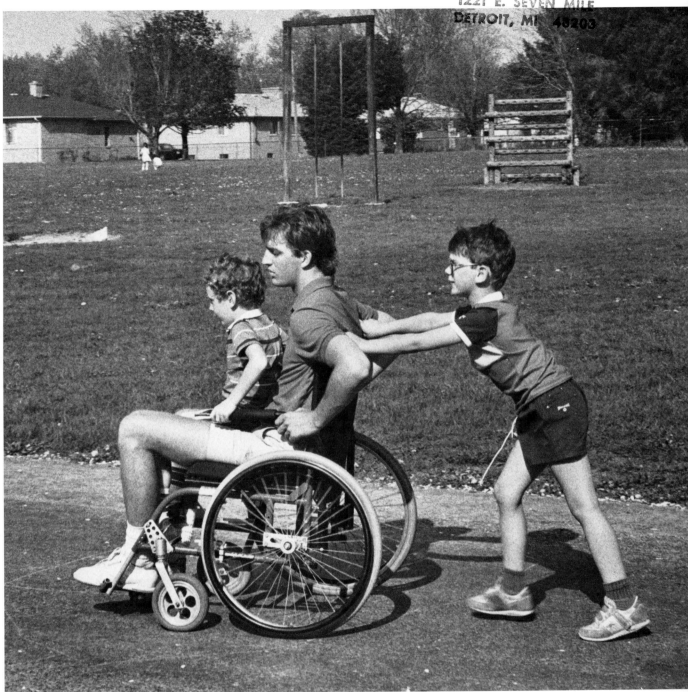

He is a teacher in a wheelchair.

When Brian was a boy, his legs were strong.
He could run in the grass, ride a bicycle,
and climb up stairs.

But when he was in college,
he was injured playing a ball game called lacrosse.
He fell to the ground and landed on his head.
He couldn't get up,
and he couldn't move his legs at all.

Brian was taken to the hospital,
where he stayed for many months.
The doctors and nurses took good care of him,
but the fall had damaged his spinal cord.
Brian's legs were partly paralyzed.
Nothing could be done to make them work
the way they did before he fell.
(Brian's injury was unusual.
Very few people are paralyzed because of a fall.)

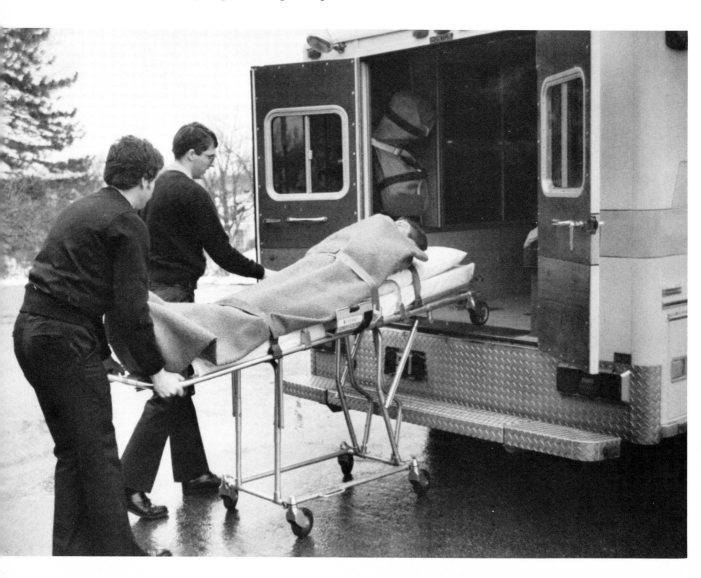

When Brian left the hospital,
he had to learn how to move in a wheelchair.
He practiced starting, steering, turning, and stopping
until he could make his way around people and things.
Now he is very good at using his wheelchair.

Brian has learned to stand and take a few steps,
but he needs his wheelchair to get from place to place.
He is tall when he stands up.

When he is in his wheelchair, he is not so tall,
and he has a lap.

Although his legs are weak and don't work well,
his arms and shoulders have grown extra-strong
from pushing the wheelchair and pulling himself up.

With his wheelchair, Brian can do most of the things he needs to do.

He has fun with his friends.

He can take care of himself.
When he is at home,
Brian cooks and does other chores
while seated in his wheelchair.

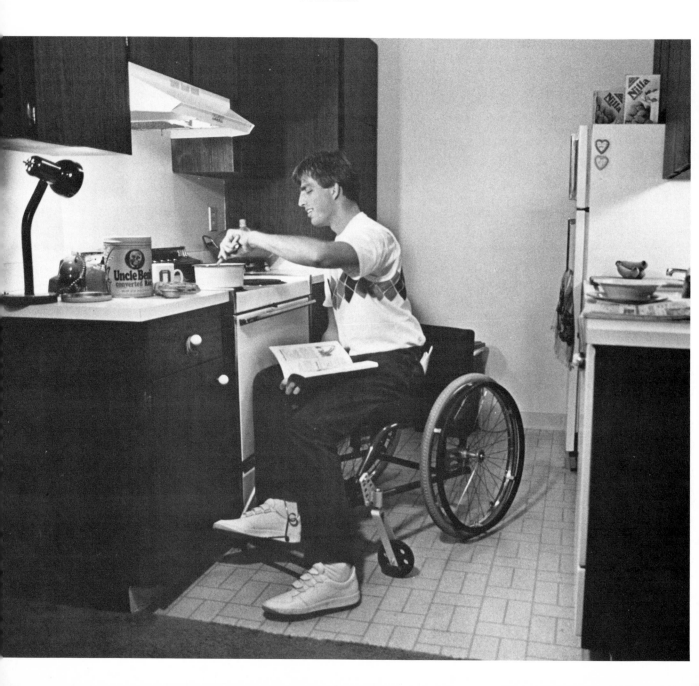

He can drive a car.
(He carries his wheelchair folded in the back seat.)

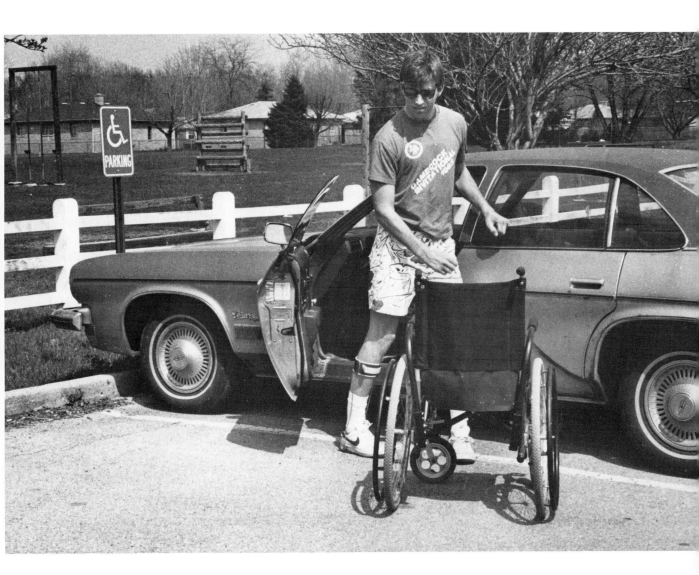

When he goes to the day-care center,
he parks his car in a special place for the handicapped.
The space is marked with a blue sign and is
close to the building, so he does not have to travel far.

At work, Brian does funny things with his wheelchair.
He plays chase and catch and "pop a wheelie."

Sometimes he lets children sit in his wheelchair
so they can take pretend space rides.

Some children are curious about Brian's
wheelchair, and some are afraid of it.
They think their legs might stop working
if they get too close to Brian or his chair.
After first meeting Brian, children often run and tumble
to make sure their legs work right.

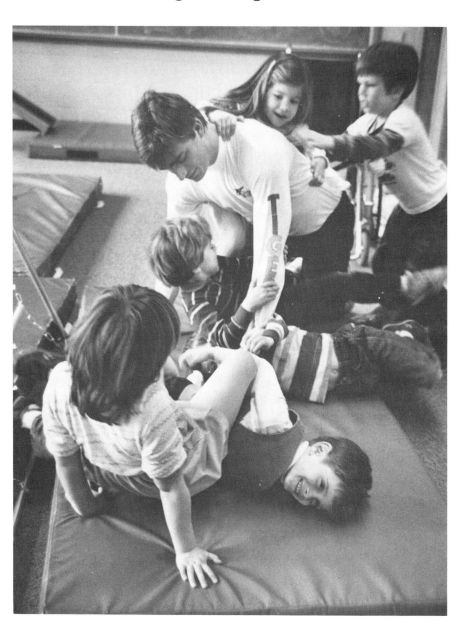

But people do not catch paralysis from each other.
It is safe to be near Brian.

Like other teachers, Brian helps children
learn, play, do their best, and be their strongest.

The children know they can count on Brian
to be there when they need him.

There are times when the children
don't like what Brian says.
Sometimes they don't want to follow his rules,
and they don't want him to tell them what to do.

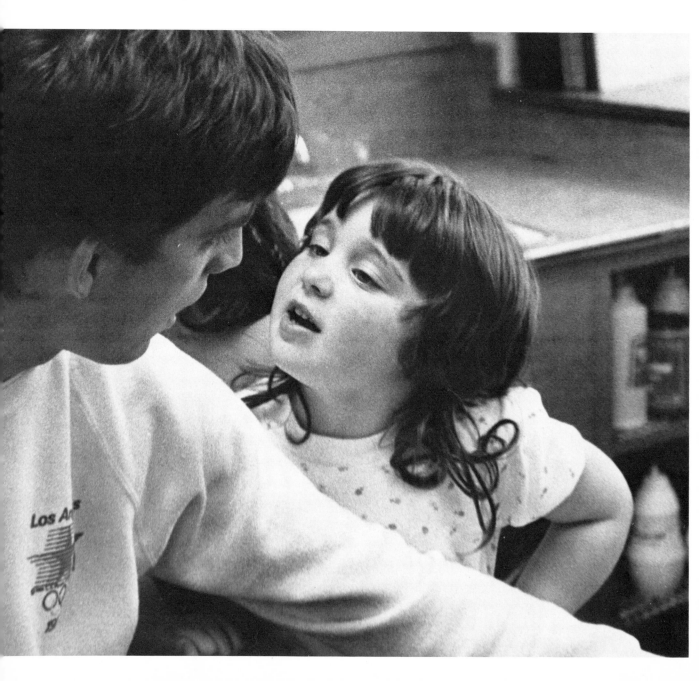

But he is the teacher.
He makes sure children listen when they need to.

Being in a wheelchair has changed Brian's life.

Sometimes he feels sad because he will never run again.
Before he was injured, running and playing ball
were Brian's favorite ways to have fun.

Brian has some problems with his wheelchair.
It can't go up and down stairs.
It is hard to get up and down curbs.
When he goes down a hill, he must stop
the spinning wheels with his hands.
Even with gloves, his hands get sore.
When it rains or snows,
his hands and gloves get wet, dirty, and cold.

His wheelchair takes up extra space
in a classroom filled with children and equipment.

Brian needs help when it is time
to put the bicycles away

or when he rides on grass or gravel.

But Brian has figured out how to live with his handicap.
He gets around almost as well as people who can walk.

When he needs help, he asks for it.
Everyone needs help with some things, some times.

This is Brian.
He knows how to take care of himself,
and other people, too.